My LAST BREATH

JVONNE BELLE

BL
Brittney LaShe'
PUBLISHING FIRM

L. Jart
Photography

Table of Contents

Dedication

This book is dedicated to....

My Mom, Joanna- You are my superwoman! You were there EVERYDAY, from the beginning all the way up until the day you all brought me home, bringing a full circle moment like the day you brought me home from the hospital as a newborn. Here I was coming home with you, with new life. Every day I opened my eyes again, because I knew you would be there. I looked forward to this each and every day. I will always be there for you. I truly would not be alive if it was not for you. Thank you, mom, for just being there.

My Dad, John-I appreciate you for being you. Everyone knows I am a daddy's girl, and your presence during this trying time exhibited the evidence of just that. When you began cracking jokes just like we used to, it made me feel alive again, even though I could not respond. You gave and continue to give me so much joy. Thanks daddy.

My Sister, Khaleelah-There are so many things I can thank you for, but most of all I thank you for being your sister's keeper. You held me down when I could not, took care of my business when I could not, and defended my honor when it was necessary. Business owners hardly ever think about being incapacitated in the prime of their business, but because of you when it happened to me, you wasted no time issuing refunds, communicating, and canceling appointments. You are an amazing sister, and I thank God for you.

My Brother, Calvin- You being near me each day, was everything I needed. You remained by my bedside and comforted me when I needed it the most. You watched over me, as my protector showing unconditional love. For that, I thank you and I will always cherish our bond.

My Daughter, Rylee-You are my reason. I love you with every part of me. Even when I could not see you, my heart beat for you. I rested in the fact that I would see you again someday. You were always at the forefront of my mind, and as you grow each day, I take pride in the young woman you are becoming. You are what I always needed in my life, and my love for you will remain constant. You are my everything Rylee, I love you.

Prologue

The 10 Second Countdown

As I take my last breath......

10....My breathing is getting slower and slower......

9....The doctors are yelling, "Grab the oxygen!"

8....My mother is yelling, "What's happening to my child?"

7....I am looking at the ceiling, my eyes are slowly closing (going in and out of consciousness)...

6.....I am thinking of my childhood, teenage years, and adulthood....

5....All the plans I have ever made and all of the people I have not said goodbye to...

4....I am now breathing slower than ever, and the breathing is deep while the exhales are long.

3....I see all of my loved ones who have crossed over.

2....I am yelling my child's name, as my spirit is lifted out of my body. I see my lifeless body....

1...Deep exhale and then...Beeeeeeeep

CHAPTER ONE

The College Drop-Out

This was not it! I was 20 years old, in my second year of college, and very unhappy. I admit that I had major plans upon arrival, but the passive aggressive discrimination was starting to get the best of me. There was no support, at least not for me. I began contemplating going home, and what I would do once I got there? I knew my parents would not be happy about this, but they had to understand that being at this predominantly white institution was not working out for me. I went through the proper withdrawal process and prepared to leave. After speaking with my parents, they informed me that although they loved me, they were not going to fully support a college drop out. I began thinking about what I was going to do before I even left, because I could not sit at home and feel like a failure every day.

With my mind on a mission to find my next, I arrived home. I began to immediately search for jobs, but I was not finding anything. No one seemed to be hiring, and it was so heartbreaking. I had no money, and I was at my parents' house. I was seemingly running out of time. I know my parents loved me, but they wanted more for me. I began considering other options, when it dawned on me: I can join the military. There I could earn income and have my college paid for. I told my parents my plan, and my mom expressed her fear, and my dad expressed his doubt. He told me I was a prissy girl, and there was no way I would cut it at basic training (although he did fully support me). His comments gave me motivation. I have always been a daddy's girl. I knew I could prove my dad wrong, because I had been an athlete all of my life. It would be nothing for me to make it through a little physical activity.

When it came to the military, I passed all of the physical tests, and met the weight requirement. I would be sent to Ft. Jackson, near my hometown to begin bootcamp, better known as Basic Training. I was extremely scared, mainly because I did not know what to expect, and once I arrived, I did not want to be there. I had always hated people telling me what to do, and the first day there I got "smoked" which is being forced to do physical activity until you all but pass out. The drill sergeant demanded that I do push-ups and I refused because at that time I couldn't fully do a push-up. She then asked me if I was slow or stupid, and I told her, "Both." She then smoked me for hours. I was mad and exhausted.

Basic was tough, but I had a lot of heart. I would bear through the worst of it, until it was just unbearable. We would have to go on these long marching walks. Once on a 10-mile walk, we were carrying 70 pounds of gear. It was so exhausting, but I was trying to make it. When we returned from the walk, I noticed that my legs had begun to swell. It was not noticeable so I figured it would go down soon enough. I laid down and rested until my night duty was to begin. Night duty was watching out for my battle buddies, making sure no one left in the middle of the night. When I woke up to begin night duty, I pushed the covers back and noticed that my legs were so swollen I could not even move them, and it looked like they were going to burst!

CHAPTER TWO

What the heck is Scleroderma?

My legs were so big, and I was so scared. I started to panic, and one of my battle buddies heard me. She rushed over and all I could say was, "My legs!" They ran to get the drill sergeants. Once they came, they picked me up and began to carry me downstairs. From there they placed me in a wheelchair and took me to medical. I was still so nervous. The medic gave me something for swelling and took x-rays. The x-rays came back normal. I was just puzzled because I had no idea what was happening to me. The doctor recommended I see a rheumatologist. After all of this was over, I was taken back to bed until the next day. While I laid there, I was still so scared, and I had no idea what a rheumatologist even was. I wondered why they wanted to send me there. My nerves were shot. I wondered if I was going to be this way forever, and was I done being able to walk. Sudden illness like this can bring about all types of thoughts.

The next morning came fast, and I was immediately taken to the rheumatologist. My mom and my grandma met us there and were in the waiting room. I was so happy to see my grandma because she was currently fighting Breast Cancer and had just left from her chemo treatment. I went in to see the doctor, and he began to look at my skin. He noticed red dots in my hands and said he thought he knew what this might be. I was relieved that somebody knew something. He did blood work and diagnosed me with scleroderma. That word was so big that it immediately placed fear in my heart, so I asked him if I was going to die. He explained to me that scleroderma is a rare autoimmune disease which caused my pigment to be the way it was because I was over-producing collagen. At that time there were only 325,000 cases documented in the United States. He asked if I was able to pinch myself and I explained to him that I was unable to pinch myself. He went on to explain what exactly scleroderma is. Scleroderma itself is a chronic hardening and contraction of the skin and connective tissue, either locally or throughout the body. There are two types of scleroderma: localized meaning it affects the skin, but sometimes affects tissues under the skin, such as muscle and bone, then there's systemic, meaning it may affect the blood circulation and internal organs as well as the skin. At that time, I was diagnosed with localized scleroderma. My body would become stiff at times, and the arthritis began to set in, in all my joints. There was no cure.

From the conversation about my diagnosis, we begin to talk about treatment options. He informed me of clinical trials, but there was not much that could be done besides slowing the progress down. Once I exited the office, I told my mom the diagnosis, but I left out several parts concerning my physical activity. I had no intentions of forgoing basic training because I had a point to prove. I was prescribed blood thinners, and before I left the office the swelling was going down. Deep down I knew my military aspirations were over because the doctor told me things would get worse. This hurt me a little bit, because it was my plan to progress within the military, but I also figured I would maintain it as long as I could. When I told my drill sergeants about what happened they all decided to support me in completing the course. They advised me to take it easy and do the bare minimum, and I figured I could work with that.

I decided I was not going to give up on my dream this easy, and I had to prove my dad wrong. Although I had a diagnosis, the military didn't even pull me out of processing. I could remain in basic as long as I could, so I was definitely going to ride this out. The male drill sergeants were very supportive of me and took it easy as promised. The female drill sergeants continued to give me hell. They felt like women were looked at as soft in the military, and they wanted to ensure that was not the case for me. I understood their point, but most days when they acted up with me, I was ready to fight.

CHAPTER THREE

Retired in my 20's

At times, the male drill sergeant would step in and them and the women would argue. They saw my dedication as a soldier, and as stated I had heart. I was glad they were able to see that in me. My leg would swell sometimes, but the blood thinners helped with the inflammation. It was still scary to see because the swelling would go over my socks, and then go back down at night. I was scared of it, but I was confident the blood thinners would do their job. When the snow began, we were scheduled to do a three-mile march. In South Carolina that year the snow got up to 5-6 inches. It was 5:00am and it was freezing cold. As we marched, I felt the circulation in my hands begin to leave. I had on two sets of gloves and hand warmers, but the warmth was not lasting. My fingers began to burn, and my hands were hurting.

The drill sergeants began to notice that something was going on with me, and I was pulled out of line. When they looked at my hand, my index finger was cracking, and something seemed to be forming. Once we arrived back, I went to medical, and they wrapped it to hold it in place. We were all preparing to go home soon for a break, and my finger was turning yellow. I knew I had to see a doctor at this point. The doctor informed me that I had frostbite, and an ulcer. They had to cut it open and let the pulse ooze out. In the process, I even lost a piece of my fingertip. I was devastated and in pain. At this point, my mom had, had it with the medical issues and told me I was not going back to basic. My dad had a sudden change of heart, and said he wanted me to go back. I think he saw my dedication and heart for what I was doing. I knew I had been diagnosed with Scleroderma, and I knew I had just lost a piece of my finger, but I still had to go back. I had to finish.

When I returned to basic, my finger was healing and in a cast. I showed the drill sergeants the video of my finger procedure. They were so grossed out, but they still commended me for continuing to come back to finish. I was blessed to have such loving leaders who cared about me. I wanted to push even more just for them. I wanted them to be proud of me. I graduated basic and made myself and my family so proud. Early into my military career I was notified that because of my medical condition, I was going to be medically retired. My career was ending as soon as it was starting. This was all bittersweet for me, because I was young and I wanted a career, but at the same time finding out I was retired at a young age with my whole life still ahead of me was also exciting. I packed up to go home and prepared for my new beginning as a retired veteran.

CHAPTER FOUR

A Grandmother's Love

After moving back home, I quickly realized that as an adult it was not feasible or accommodating for me to remain in my parents' home. I moved into an apartment with my boyfriend at the time and we started our life together. I had always been heavily involved in the church, under the influence of my grandmother Rachel. I was in the choir, and I attended Bible study faithfully. I loved church, and I loved learning about who God is, and how important it is that He is always a part of my life. I was enjoying my independence while also working at the V.A. as a valet. I knew at some point I needed to figure out what I really wanted to do with my life. I wanted to do something to make my grandmother really proud of me. I knew she already was, but I wanted to do something more.

My grandma was still battling breast cancer at this time. For years prior to my grandmother's diagnosis, she had felt a lump but never truly worried about it. It wasn't until the lump started bothering her, that she got it checked out. Finally, my grandmother went to the doctor where they performed a biopsy. After the biopsy they determined it was breast cancer. By the time they found it, it had spread. Her breast would need to be removed, and she would be able to beat it. After about a year of being cancer free, it returned. We were all heartbroken by this. To make matters even worse, the cancer had spread to her brain this time. I could not come to terms with what was happening to my grandmother.

Within eight months, my grandmother's decline was happening rapidly. It hurt me so much to see it. One day I visited her, and took her, her favorite hotdog. I was so excited to give it to her, and I wanted us to enjoy the hotdogs together. When I arrived, she was holding her head down. I still tried to cheer her up, because I knew again that this was her favorite. She took one bite of the hotdog and began to vomit. She was suffering, and it broke my heart. I stepped outside and broke down crying. I was just hurt all over. A few weeks after that she suffered a stroke. She went into the hospital, and never left after that. I lost my best friend, my ride or die, and my right hand. In her eyes, I could do no wrong. We were each other's everything. She was my girl for real!

After losing my grandmother. I felt different. Life just seemed unfair. At this time, I had lost both of my grandmothers two months apart. I know God knew they were my everything so I could not understand why He would take them both. I needed them, especially my grandma Rachel.

The girl I once was, who thirsted for every ounce of God, was upset with Him. I left the church, because I no longer saw the point. How could I worship, when I could not even understand my own emotions, and how I could heal from them? As I write this, I am still grieving my grandmothers. Our family is so big, and we all were hurting due to Grandma Rachel's loss, it felt like my emotions got lost somehow. I wanted to be strong for them, but deep down I was suffering. As I watched my grandmother's casket be lowered into the ground, truth be told, I wanted to go with her. My heart was so heavy after that, because I loved her so much. One day I realized I needed to get up and figure out my life, because I needed to do something to honor my grandmother.

CHAPTER FIVE

Unpretty

Education had always been important to my grandmother. She would speak about it all the time and speak life into my educational goals. As a child, she was always proud of my grades, and the fact that I was an honor student. She often reminded me that I was special, and I would go far in life. At the time of her passing none of her grandchildren had graduated college yet, and I am the oldest granddaughter, so the ball was certainly in my court. I made the decision to make her proud and enroll back in school. I was not only doing this for her, but this was for me as well. I had to succeed this time. It was personal.

I enrolled in a 2-year college, Aiken Tech, using my G.I. Bill. I was blessed to have school paid for in spite of my career being over. During that time, I found out from my doctor that it would not be safe for me to carry a child. I was devastated. They explained that my skin would need to stretch, and because of my illness that may cause major issues, because my skin did not stretch as it should. This caused me so many emotions. The thought that I would never be a mom, broke my heart. Finding this out also made me curious. Who else was living with this condition? How was it affecting their skin? Did they have children? I went on social media and found a support group called *Scleroderma Warriors*. It was comforting to know there were others out there.

In the support group people posted pictures of their skin and discussed their reactions to trial medications. They would post before and after photos. I admired them for their bravery. After really looking at their skin, I realized that I looked like these people. We all looked the same, with the same features. The condition caused our lips to shrink inward, and not appear full like they once were. Our noses were slimmer, and our eyes had dark spots. The skin pulling was also obvious. This was insane to me. I could not believe that condition could make us all so similar. Our fingertips and toes were even the same with ulcers. You could also identify the areas of our joints that suffered from arthritis. Although this was scary and weird, it gave me a sense of peace to know I was not the only one out there.

Another reason finding the group was so comforting was the fact that I had begun to become ashamed of how I looked. In high school, I was what people called an "it girl." My self-esteem was high, I loved being around people, and the boys were always checking for me. Now here I was, hiding myself. As I continued to look at images in the group, I noticed many of the conditions of the other people were worse than mine. In my mind I began to think that this was going to happen to me soon. I was so depressed about it all. The impending doom stayed with me every day, and the suicidal thoughts begin to creep into my mind. I questioned why this was happening to me. I barely ever went without makeup. Even my live-in boyfriend rarely saw me without makeup. There were moments when I started to leave the house with him without makeup, that he kind of made it known to me that he would rather me wear it. This stung a little, but I figured he was doing the best he could, dealing with my condition and all. I felt that I could not expect him to just ignore it. People talk about inner beauty all the time, but not everyone is adaptable to that concept. I mean at this point my face had turned white!

I begin to go deeper into a dark place. I was hurting so bad, and I felt so sorry for myself. I knew society had a view on how we should look, and I knew inner beauty had nothing to do with it. Magazines had been setting the standard for beauty for decades, and now social media made it even worse. Everywhere we looked, we needed to look better than the next person. My grandma always spoke affirmations of beauty into my life. She reminded me of how pretty I was, and she also reminded me to never allow anyone to tell me otherwise. She literally made sure my crown was never crooked. Now, I did not feel that at all. My depression became deeper. Truth be told, I felt ugly. I stopped even wearing makeup. I figured I may as well let how I look overtake me since it was bound to happen sooner or later.

My biggest step at this time was going out in public without any makeup. People would see me and ask what was wrong. Sometimes my fingertips had ulcers on them and open sores. I wanted to just be silent and go about my day, but I knew people needed this knowledge. I would tell them that I had a rare autoimmune disease called scleroderma. I explained to them how it affected my skin, and even how it made my skintight. People became very interested in it and asked even more questions. They began to show their genuine concern, and I felt so much love. Soon people close to me begin researching doctors to find help for me. This was refreshing to know that people cared this much about me. My confidence was becoming restored.

CHAPTER SIX

A Mommy with a Degree

My boyfriend and I continued on as we were, and I eventually stopped thinking about getting pregnant or being a mom at all. I was focused on school and building a life for myself. One day I woke up feeling terrible. I just knew I was having another flare up. I was so tired of this, and plus this flare up felt very different. I was vomiting so bad. I decided to just go to the emergency room to get checked out, because none of this was normal. When we arrived, they ran several tests, and the nurse asked me if I could be pregnant. I quickly told her "no." I figured since they told me I did not need to have children; my body was handling that. The nurse left to get an update on the test they ran and came back and told me I was in fact pregnant, and my due date was my grandmother's birthday. I knew she was there, but I was also devastated. I had no idea how my body would handle any of this. I was told to take vitamins and rest.

As life would have it, the next nine months were amazing for me. My pregnancy was easy going, and I had never felt better. I was so grateful for my body, for the first time in a while. It did exactly what it was supposed to do to prepare itself for motherhood. I kept myself moisturized to eliminate any chances of a scleroderma flare up. It was an amazing experience. In the latter part I did end up with gallstones, and I delivered prematurely. My baby girl was and still is a beautiful gift from God and a reminder of His grace and mercy. My life was changed at the moment, and I knew I needed to focus on bringing her up in love, and making sure I was prepared.

As a new mom, I decided to go back to school and work towards earning my bachelor's degree. During this time, I decided not to work, and just stay at home while living off of my military benefits. I was feeling pretty good health wise and was only on blood thinners and ibuprofen. The doctors were recommending that I enter into various clinical trials, but I denied them because from reading the post in the Facebook support group, I begin to see some decline as a result of participating in the trials. I decided to spare myself those troubles and focus on what was making me feel better. My parents were happy to be grandparents, and I was happy for them. Truth be told, they were not as excited about my relationship, but I desired for my daughter to have a family. The stress of trying to maintain that happy home, did contribute to my flare ups at times.

Toward the end of me earning my bachelor's degree my relationship was really on the rocks, but I was too busy to focus on that. I had gone back to work at this time as well. I knew my daughter was watching me, and she was witnessing me work nights, and go to school during the day. She would ask about my books when she saw them, and wanted to know what I was doing with them. I explained to her that I was in school, and soon she would be going too. When I completed my degree, it was such a happy time. My daughter and my family were there, and that is what mattered most. I was not going to allow anything to take that day away from me. As I marched in, I heard my baby yell, "Mommy!" My family was screaming as well. I was crying so hard. I knew grandma was watching me, and I wanted her to know we did it.

CHAPTER SEVEN

Another Level

I earned my Bachelor of Science in business management. My goal was to find a fulfilling job and purchase a home for me and my daughter. At this point I was still working, but not my dream job as of yet. I was off blood thinners and was maintaining my health by taking ibuprofen only. As a working mom now, I was even more grateful for the support I had with my daughter. I did not have to worry about who would take care of her while I worked. This was such a relief. As far as my pain went, I felt some type of pain daily. The ibuprofen made it easier to manage. There was also some form of inflammation at all times as well. I experienced no major significant changes during this season, good or bad. I was just "okay" and I made it work. The doctor at one point, recommended a chemotherapy pill, but I was not willing to take that either. I was just not interested in placing more chemicals in my body when I was doing fine almost naturally.

One day while holding my daughter, she began to rub my face. She pointed at a particular spot on my face and said "mama." At that moment, I knew she noticed that there was something different there. I desired to be open with her, and not try to hide things, so I explained to her what it was. She always wanted to rub my face. She is so loving. I used this moment as a teachable moment for her. We talked about skin tones and race, and how to treat people. I wanted to be real with her. I wanted her to love her skin. I believed in raising a little girl to love herself regardless of her skin tone or hair texture.

I have continued to talk to my daughter about how she looks while reminding her of how beautiful she is. I have also prepared her for the world, which can sometimes be very cruel. I told her that people may talk about her, but she can't allow their words to affect her. She must continue to keep her head held high and walk in confidence. I remind her that she is a princess. My affirmations into her life are instilled in her, and she knows these things are true.

During my time as an undergrad, I was informed of a job that really interested me. My current job did not pay well, plus I worked overnights. I applied for the other job twice with my associate degree but was denied both times. I felt terrible about this, because I really would have liked to have that job, but by the second denial, I felt that it was not for me. I was encouraged to apply a third time, although I did not really want to. I went ahead and applied, and in January 2018 I received the job. I was so excited; I was crying tears of joy. This job is not easy for most people to attain with a Bachelors, so I was so proud of myself. I knew I interviewed well because I went in as myself. I did not try to overdo it or impress them. I wanted them to see me authentically. I had a conversation with them, and they were impressed with that. I could not believe I was about to be employed with the largest payroll processing company in the world. Within the first seven months I received my first promotion, and from the beginning I was told that, that only happens after the first 18 months. That was a favor.

CHAPTER EIGHT

All Things New

The company began to teach me everything about how a business operates. I appreciated the knowledge. I had never thought much about starting a business, but all of the training was so eye-opening. It was so refreshing to be walking into a new environment. My baby was starting school soon, I was flourishing at my new job, my relationship was not in the best place still, but the lease was almost up at the apartment, so that meant transition as well. I decided I was not going to try and get another apartment to force my relationship to work. I knew I wanted a home of my own, so my daughter and I moved back home with my parents so I could save and purchase one.

I was giving myself a year to save for my home. I knew I could do it, because I was determined, and just about anything I put my mind to I could accomplish it. I began to focus on saving the money we needed and using my spare time to perfect my makeup and build my own confidence. People begin to become very forward about commenting on my makeup. They would even go as far as to ask me to do theirs, but I was not sure about that. I liked doing my makeup, and I loved how it made me look and feel, but I was not sure about doing others. Since they asked though, I began to practice on my little sister. She was willing to be my guinea pig, and I needed to be sure I could do this. Once I started with her, people continued to ask so I started accepting clients.

I started accepting makeup booking for $30 and beating faces (doing make-up) right in my mother's dining room. I had become an entrepreneur overnight. As 2018 was coming to a close more things began to look up for me. By November I was officially building my home. It took me less than a year to get that plan off the ground. I felt unstoppable. I had a degree, a great job, a business, and I was as healthy as I could be. In April my daughter and I moved into our newly built home. My business continued to grow right after that. As 2019 rolled in, I officially deemed myself an MUA (make-up artist). I was booking proms, weddings, birthday parties, and all types of gatherings. My confidence was at an all-time high. I loved every ounce of what I was doing, and the woman I was becoming. Me, who had once felt so down about myself, was now in the business of making others feel beautiful. God truly has a sense of humor.

Although there were so many great things happening for me, I still could not find my way back to God. Everything was happening fast too. I knew it was Him moving in my life, but I struggled to forge that relationship. I knew His hands were always on my life, but I kept my distance. I also knew He wanted me to know my grandmother was near. My house number is 591 and my grandma's funeral was on 09-15. Those subtle signs were still showing up. Once we were settled into our home, my daughter transferred to a new school. She was flourishing in school. She was also winning beauty pageants and making friends. I was so proud of my baby. I was once again promoted at my job, and things just continued to improve.

CHAPTER NINE

Staying Focused in a Pandemic

When I think of my health in those seasons, I only remember stability, and because my health was so stable, I needed everything in my life to be that way. Of course there was day to day pain, but I managed all of that very well. I felt in control, and relatively normal. I was happy, at my healthiest in a long time, a boss, and winning in my career. My daughter was confident and so sweet. I was so proud of her and just grateful for my own growth as a woman and a mother.

My doctor appointments were still regular, but I was not happy with my old rheumatologist at the time. He was just very laid back. He never ran any blood work, and I did not know much about my status. He would send medicine in the mail, but I wanted to know why he was prescribing these medicines. I could not get a clear answer, and I am sure with no blood work he did not have one. I did not trust him, so I never took any of that medicine. I continued with my ibuprofen routine, and I trusted that. My condition always reminded me it was there, but I had to keep going. My family was proud of me because I was letting nothing stop me. Not scleroderma, not a relationship, nothing. I was doing things in my family that would change generations. I had a degree and built a house from the ground up. My body felt good and there were no changes.

When we began to enter into 2020 there was word that an uncommon virus had broken out in China. People were warned to steer clear of the area, and the CDC was keeping a watchful eye on the spread of the disease and how to combat it. At the end of 2019 it was business as usual. People were traveling but every now and then you would hear of someone dying from an upper respiratory infection. No one thought much about it though. Historically there was always some type of disease threatening to enter the United States, but it never really did. I was not worried. As 2020 came though, the warnings got stronger. People were getting nervous. It was not long before we were hearing that this virus, COVID-19 had entered the U.S. The first known case was here, and it was not looking good. It was not long after that, that it entered my state, and now everything was on high alert. Basically, in March of 2020 the world came to a halt.

I soon found out that research showed that people with weakened immune systems, or auto-immune diseases of any kind needed to be extra careful. I took my health seriously. I let my makeup clients know I could no longer accept them. My child was now at home with me, my job had sent us all home to work, and we hunkered down. I was extra careful everywhere I went and normally wore two masks. For the next five months, I didn't do any makeup and rarely allowed anyone in my home at all. I admit I was nervous, but I had to stay focused. After the five-month period, I decided to start back taking clients but with heavy restrictions. They would need to show a negative test result taken within 24 hours and clean themselves thoroughly before entering. I would even clean even more after each appointment.

By now my daughter had begun kindergarten, and it hurt me that she had to start at home. I was having to work from home, and work with her on the zoom with her teacher. This was beyond difficult. Every so often when the students did not understand something, the teacher would say "Get your helper" and that was me. I tried my best not to be frustrated about it, but I knew my baby needed to be in school. I was doing my best to help her with her work and pay attention to what was going on at my job. This was our routine every day. It was so stressful, but we made it. During the weekdays I was pretty much on my own with her, but I did have support from my family on the weekends. In the midst of all of this stress though, I was still in good health.

Clients had begun booking consistently, so when one particular client booked me, I was not concerned. She sent in her negative test results, and we were good to go. Once she arrived at the appointment, she began to cough. I immediately put my guard up and asked her if she was okay. She explained that she suffered from allergy issues. I accepted that and kept working, because I also had on two masks and gloves. She continued to cough though. I stopped her process and told her she needed to leave. I understood that she claimed to have allergies, but I could not put myself at risk. She left without her makeup done. The very next day, I woke up feeling terrible, and I immediately knew I could not taste or smell. I was so scared. I knew what it was, and I knew who had given it to me. It was insane how fast this virus permeated my body and took over. I took an at-home test, and it was positive. I was so hurt. I had no idea what this virus would do to me. From there I went to the doctor the next day to be sure, and sure enough I was positive with COVID-19.

CHAPTER TEN

A First-Class Life

I could not believe this evil thing had caught up with me! Of course there were no medications to treat COVID-19, people were just instructed to remain in isolation, drink hot teas and lemon water, and rest. I also took cough syrup in hopes of speeding up my recovery. My daughter went with her father and his aunt during this time, as well as my mom. I missed her, but I knew it was important that she remained safe. While getting everything squared away, I could not stop thinking about the girl who brought this virus into my home. I texted her and told her I had COVID to see what she would say. She told me she was sorry, because she really needed her makeup done for an event later that night. She then admitted to using her cousin's negative results. I was so mad. How could she be so irresponsible and careless with my life? I realized then that people truly don't care when it comes to what they want. In this world, you must look out for yourself.

I was instructed to take COVID test weekly to monitor my status. I decided that I was closing my make-up business again for a while, at least for the remainder of the year. I needed to completely recover, get my house in order, and re-focus. I just needed time. Once 2021 started things were back in motion. My daughter was going back to school and was set to have a somewhat real kindergarten experience. I was happy for her. I wanted her to make sure she wore her mask, because it was important to her and mommy's health. She understood, and understood a little too well. I began receiving calls from her teachers telling me they had to beg her to take her mask off just to eat. I then intervened and let my baby know that she needed to take it off to eat, but I appreciated her looking out for me the way she did. I felt that she was so sweet and thoughtful. I knew then that I was raising a force.

As soon as 2021 came in, I began seeing the blessings on the other side of a very hard year. A lady reached out to me about needing makeup. Someone referred me to her, but unfortunately, I could not do her makeup that day. She went on to tell me that in spite of her not being able to book an appointment with me she loved my responsiveness. She went on to say she had heard so many great things about me, she wanted to do something for me. She informed me that she was a talent agent from Los Angeles, and she had a gig in Hollywood that she wanted me to be a part of. I was ecstatic. I was really being invited to L.A. due to my make-up talent. The same talent I was unsure of, and the same girl that had been so insecure about her skin. I was in total shock. She went on to tell me that they would cover my flight, and they were willing to pay me $4,500.00. I was in complete awe.

Once I was done with the conversation, and accepted the assignment I contacted my friend who lived in L.A. She was a physical therapist, and I knew she would not have a problem with me staying with her. I was in heavy anticipation of the experience. I was grateful for my career that provided me with leave and vacation days I could take. Once I arrived, I was informed that I would only be required to work two hours per day on a film and magazine set. I was about to meet some amazing, up and coming people in the industry. The work environment was super-fast paced, and the models and actors only wanted the bare minimum of makeup on their faces. Man, to think that I went from taking my first clients in my mom's dining room to this, still shocks me today. I developed content while there to continue to promote my business and enjoyed sightseeing in the city with my friend. I knew then that a life of luxury is certainly accessible to us, we just have to do the work. Once I returned from this experience, I was booking clients left and right!

CHAPTER ELEVEN

The Vaccine

Within the year 2021, I booked 27 weddings alone. I was being invited to fashion shows, and even flew to New York to work one. I had to pinch myself, because I could not believe this was my life. I was a whole brand. A friend from college who was a musician was able to connect me with the New York fashion show. Health wise I felt amazing, and my daughter was flourishing. We were still in the pandemic, but I was doing fine with maintaining my health and staying out of danger. I was glad that fear did not keep me bound and keep me from taking advantage of these grand opportunities. I was learning, growing, and becoming someone I could be even more proud of.

As the pandemic raged on, there had been word that a few companies were working on a vaccine. These vaccines would not rid us of the virus, but if everyone did their part and took them, we could decrease the spread. This was a situation kind of like chicken pox. At a certain time in history, a vaccine for chickenpox came about, and if you pay attention, we begin to deal with a society that either had, had chicken pox or had the vaccine. So now we rarely hear of a case, and if we do it is few and far between. This was the plan for COVID-19 in relation to the vaccine. We were still consistently wearing masks, but they were pushing people to take this vaccine. I was leery of it. I was reading, and I knew there were two different brands. They both had their own side effects. The vaccine was to be taken in two doses, a week or so apart.

Due to my autoimmune disease, I truly did not want to take the vaccine at all. I was not sure what it would do to my body, or how it could counteract with what I had. I was in a good place, and very stable. I rarely even had any doctor's appointments. Remember, I had relied on pain relievers as I lived with scleroderma. I was not one to put chemicals into my body that I felt were unnecessary. As time progressed the pressure to get the vaccine got worse. We begin to get notices at work that the vaccine was going to become mandatory for us. There was a ruling that began to allow companies to do this. Once I heard this, I was not happy, but I loved my job, so I went ahead and scheduled it.

Once I told my doctor I was planning to take the vaccine, he was excited. I was not sure if the excitement was for me or for the fact that they were getting people to buy into this vaccine. If you pay attention, every time you visit the doctor they offer something like a flu shot or tetanus shots. I took the first shot in October. I anticipated any strange feelings I may have. For the most part I felt fine, but I noticed when I went to the gym to work out two days later, even after an intense workout, I did not break a sweat. I normally sweat profusely, so that was very strange. I wrote it off as just a weird occurrence. Two weeks after that though, I had swelling in my legs and face, coupled with migraines. I called my doctor, because I was worried at this point. He instructed me to just take some ibuprofen, so I did.

The second shot was scheduled for November. Earlier that year, after traveling so much with various opportunities, and having a successful year, I figured it was time I planned my two dream vacations: Costa Rica and Greece. I was so excited and looking forward to doing what I had dreamed of doing for so long. When January of 2022 came in, I was focused, and my mind was on my trips. In the midst of my excitement though I began to become short of breath and the inflammation continued to take place. On-top of this I was still not sweating at the gym, and the migraines had become very intense. The migraines got so bad that my hair turned gray in the center of my head.

CHAPTER TWELVE

Something is Different

At this time, not only was my breathing getting shorter, I just felt different. It was hard for me to describe, but it was not like the slight pain I felt on the regular, it was just a different feeling. Because of how I felt, I noticed I began to move slower. I had to take my time doing things, and I had become so tired, I could barely work out. This had been a part of my normal routine, so it was very strange. The swelling in my hands and face continued, it was like my past was hunting me. I did not understand it. It had been so long since I had dealt with any of this. I was confused and upset about why this was even happening to my body. I decided to go to the ER before we left, just to ensure everything was okay. I knew Costa Rica was coming up very soon, and I was doing all I could to get back on my feet before then. The doctor prescribed me medicine for the swelling and sent me home. My college bestie and I had heard so many things about Costa Rica, and my travel agent had a great deal on this trip. It had been booked since 2021, so we were all geared up to go.

The week before my trip I did not feel well at all. Luckily, I had a high pain tolerance, but I knew I had to be somewhat in good health to leave the country. My friend from college was traveling with me, and she was so patient and loving. We had major plans to party hard, explore, and eat great food. I gave Costa Rica all I had. There were amazing beach views, island tours, ATV riding, hiking a volcano, mud baths, great local food, zip lining, and so much more. My friend Dawn was asking if I was okay, because she noticed I had a yellowish look on my face. I told her it must have just been the heat having an effect on my skin. I was moving so slower than normal the entire trip. I was trying to push myself to keep going and keep enjoying, but it was so hard. By the time I reached home, my face was swollen even more.

Once I arrived home, ulcers began to form in the top of my mouth and at the bottom of my feet. I was distraught. The migraines were more intense than ever, and the swelling had gotten worse. I was running a fever, and my breathing was a little weak. It was like I was truly reliving things that happened to me years before. I checked into the emergency room for the second time for the relatively same symptoms. They examined me and prescribed me vitamins and prednisone for it. Prednisone mainly treats inflammation. They did not take any blood work, but performed CT Scans and said they did not see anything abnormal. This was now June, and my trip to Greece was scheduled for July. My college besties and I had planned to see Greece when we reached our 30's. I loved Greek mythology and had read books on Greece my entire life. I was even in tune with the culture and history of the country. Everything was covered and I just did not want to miss this trip. I continued with my plans in spite of the fact that now the ulcers in my mouth and on my feet made it difficult for me to eat and walk. It all burned.

I returned to the ER for the third time, because I wanted to ensure I did not have COVID or the flu before leaving the country. I knew scleroderma was not causing these symptoms. I had been living with that for so long, and I knew what those flare ups looked and felt like. Once again, I was prescribed pain medication and was told that this was just another flare up. I told them during that visit that I knew something was wrong with my body, and things had been like this since I took those shots. I tried my best to focus on enjoying Greece, but I was getting worse by the day. We planned to shop, take beautiful pictures of the artifacts and architecture. Along with those wonderful experiences, we also took a six-mile bike history excursion through Athens, ate great food, did a boat ride which stopped at three different islands, and learned even more history. We laid out on the beach in Santorini (and took a day flight there) and saw the infamous blue top buildings. I was able to participate in all activities once again, and I was so pleased.

Although I was pleased that I was able to enjoy Greece, I admit that I was miserable the entire time. I could not walk for long periods due to the ulcers on my feet. I could not enjoy the amazing food due to the ulcers in my mouth. My friends Talea and Dawn felt so sorry for me, because when they wanted to go out at night, I would be in bed in so much pain, trying to fall asleep. I did not want to be a burden to them although they cared for me. I tried my best not to complain. I did not want to ruin the trip for anybody. I did my best to suck up the pain and keep it moving. My breathing became more shallow during the trip but thank God this did not start until the last full day. As we began the long trek back to Atlanta, I could feel my body shutting down. I could not eat or walk for long periods of time. I could not believe any of this was happening to me. Lymph nodes begin to poke out from my neck. There were nine of them poking out by the time we arrived in Italy. At that point I knew my body was fighting an infection, but I had no idea what kind or what caused it.

My friends were scared, and I was just tired. They knew something was very wrong. In Italy there was a six-hour layover. I was so exhausted. They went to try to find food and medicine, and even a wheelchair, but they weren't able to find one for me. I was getting worse, and my friends were starting to realize I may need to go to the hospital. I was adamant that I was not going to a hospital in a foreign country. I was crying and praying for an ounce of relief. The hospital there would not have my records and I could not run the risk of not receiving the proper care, due to the doctors not knowing my medical history. When it was finally time to board the flight to Atlanta, it was to be 11 hours long. I was dreading it from the start, but I knew I needed to get on U.S. soil before I could get treatment.

CHAPTER THIRTEEN

Everything Went Black

On the 11-hour flight home, I was in so much pain. Luckily, I was in comfort class so I was as comfortable as I could be. I was antsy and moving around a whole lot in the seat. I still could not eat, and they were just giving me ice. Once we arrived in Atlanta, I realized I could not just go straight home. I had been in a relationship that ended recently, but my ex's daughter Trinity (who's my daughter as well) and I were still so close. She would come visit me and stay solely with me and my daughter. I value our relationship. The next day she was set to arrive in Atlanta, and I needed to pick her up, so I spent the night at my ex's brother's house so I could make sure I got her. I did not sleep at all that night. All of this had been pre-planned and I always needed to follow through. That night he picked her up for me. From there we drove from Atlanta back to South Carolina. She was a teenager, so she knew I was hurting. It was only supposed to take a little over two hours to get home, but it took me over three hours due to the pain. In case you are wondering how I was able to do all of this, for years I had developed an extremely high pain tolerance. When a task was before me, regardless of my condition I had learned to see things through if I could.

Once I arrived in South Carolina I went straight to the ER, for the fourth time. They did another CT Scan, and once again said they did not see anything. While at home, my daughter and my stepdaughter were trying their best to take care of me. I was sleeping most of the day away and my family was bringing me food. They were not aware that I had been back and forth to the ER for months. I appreciated these babies and my family for helping me, because I was not feeling well at all. Soon my stepdaughter's mom arrived to take her back to Texas, and I was still in pain, and feeling sick. As I was battling this, I also had a wedding scheduled in Atlanta and needed to do makeup for eight people. I had felt slightly better a few days before this, so I thought I would be fine to go. I had waited too late and did not get a chance to cancel it. I woke up at 3:00am, because I was moving so slow, I needed the extra time. When I arrived at the hotel, I was almost ready to pass out. I sat in the car for a while before even going in. I drove down, did her wedding and as I was preparing to leave the lymph nodes were poking out of my neck again. When I returned back home (July 31st), I went back to the ER (this was now the fifth time) and they once again did a CT scan, gave me meds, and sent me home.

As time progressed, my birthday was coming (August 2nd). I hated to be sick on my birthday, but I was just willing to deal with it. My friend Noel came over to take me out to eat as he always did. I was not prepared for this, so I laid on the couch to try to wrap my head around it. I also had a photoshoot and makeup appointment scheduled for later that day. He and I began to have a conversation about various things, and in the middle of the conversation, I realized that I could not breathe. He was still talking and had not yet noticed. I finally looked at him and said, "I can't breathe." He jumped and called 911. I felt like I was dying. By now my sister was walking in with my birthday present, she immediately recognized the situation. She grabbed my daughter and took her to my friend/neighbor's house, so she did not have to witness the ambulance arriving. I am so glad she did that, as I wanted to always ensure my daughter was protected from trauma.

Once the ambulance arrived, my oxygen had dropped below 50. I felt like I was about to code. They rushed me to the hospital. I was so scared and in so much pain. Once I arrived, I could see my mom was in the room. This was comforting, but I still could not breathe. Hospital staff were coming in looking at me, but it did not appear that anyone was doing anything. My mom was agitated, and she was yelling. She needed someone to do something to help me. I felt so helpless and hopeless. I laid there hoping someone would do something to help me. Finally, after several hours, I remembered seeing a doctor rush in the room stating my lungs had collapsed and I needed to be placed on life support. I remember thinking about my clients and sending back their deposit, I began refunding payments and even wrote a few text messages telling people about me going on life support, yeah, I know crazy right? At that point I was immediately placed on life support, and everything went black.

43

CHAPTER FOURTEEN

It Moved

The doctors began to work on me, but they couldn't figure out for the life of them what caused my lungs to collapse and all of my organs to inflame. They said they did see bacterial pneumonia, but there appeared to be something more happening. Because they were at a loss, and I was now on life support, they explained to my mother that they were unsure if I would make it through. At this point they were just preparing to put me on dialysis. There was one doctor that my mom eventually told me, paced the floor daily, because he could not figure out what was wrong with me. My mom decided that she would not just let me stay there and die. A nurse came around and told my mom that if she wanted me to live to get me out of there. She gave her two hospitals that she believed could save my life. From there my mother instructed them to move me to another hospital. The transfer process began and after two weeks, I was transported by ambulance to a different hospital. The original plan was to airlift me, but the weather was too bad. Once at the next hospital, I was placed on the extracorporeal membrane oxygenation (ECMO). This is a machine that takes over the heart and lung function when the patient's organs do not work on their own. All of my organs were inflamed and had begun to shut down. My mother was told that if I did not respond to the machine in 14 days, I would be taken off and they would have to prepare for my departure from this life.

For the next two weeks I laid there. From what I was told multiple tests were run. A special team of rheumatologists had come in to research my situation. They ran more blood work. They knew that my symptoms were different and did not align with anything I had been diagnosed with. As they continued to run more tests, take more blood, and research, they finally discovered the culprit: I had lupus. They informed my mom. My head was swollen, my brain was swollen, I had a stroke, hemorrhaging on the brain, and I had seizures. This was all while in a coma. At this time my daughter only knew that I was in the hospital. She did not have any other details, and she was not brought to see me. Again, I appreciated my family for stepping in and avoiding subjecting my daughter to trauma.

There were so many machines' people could not even really get inside the room. While in my coma there were no dreams, and I did not hear anything. My best friends came and documented my condition. They would record themselves telling me the latest gossip, and pretending as if I was engaging. Mom was there every single day for at least 13 hours per day, 8:00am-9:00pm. There were so many people coming to see me (one doctor told my mom I must be someone of importance from all the people coming), and I am sure the condition I was in was unexpected and shocking to them. Once they would be allowed in, some of them were passing out from what they saw. For 13 days as my mom stayed and watched, the machine never moved. I know she prayed, and she talked to me, but there was no activity. Nothing happened, and with each passing day things were looking grim. Truth is, while in the coma I just remember staring in the dark hoping that a light would come on.

On the fourteenth day, all of the doctors came in. They informed my parents that they had done all they could and had even come to a diagnosis. The issue was I was not showing any activity or responding to the machine. They let her know that as she had been informed, and they were now at 14 days, and it was a matter of time before I would need to be taken off the machine. My mom and dad were heartbroken. This is what we had come to and what she prayed would not happen. The doctor went on to explain that once I would be taken off the machine, I would proceed to transition at that point on my own. At that moment my parents broke down, and as the word transition slid off the doctor's tongue, the vitals on the machine moved.

CHAPTER FIFTEEN

Awake

The doctors were shocked, they said "Wait, it moved! We have movement!" My mom went into a moment of worship. No one can tell us what God can't do. My mom's praise began to go beyond excitement to the point that she had to be removed from the room so the medical team could work. After they studied the movement, they told her they would be running more tests and reviewing the situation. There was hope, and that is what we needed. To my mom, she knew it could only get better. My family and friends waited for more news, and at this time the best news was that I would not be coming off of the ECMO because of death, but eventually I would be coming off because of progress.

The very next morning, I opened my eyes. I was immediately ready to start talking, then I realized I could not. I was beyond afraid. There were tubes down my throat, a trach in my neck, and I could not move. I was paralyzed. All I could do was blink, and I was also confused. I realized the hospital looked different from when I first was placed in a coma, I was not sure why, but I could hear and comprehend. After a while, my mom walked in, and I heard her say, "Good Morning Jvonne!" But she did not look at me right away. I was thinking "Look up Ma, Look up!" When she finally looked at me, she saw my eyes were open. She started yelling immediately. As soon as the yelling started, my dad came in. He was shocked and excited as well. I was getting excited with them, and the machine started to beep. My mom told me to calm down. I tried to, but I needed so many answers.

The doctors finally came in and began to explain everything. They told me I was paralyzed, and they were unsure if I would ever move my body, let alone walk again. I immediately began having anxiety about this information. If I was going to be paralyzed to the point of only blinking, truth be told, I did not want to live. I wanted to be the person I was before any of this happened. I know it may sound selfish to some, but this is how I truly felt. I begin to cry. My feelings were so hurt. They began to run various tests telling me to blink once or twice, to answer the questions they were asking me. They continued to explain what had happened to me. There were marks on my arm that told me that I had been restrained. They explained that I once woke up and began pulling at things. They could not run the risk of me pulling a tube out that would cause bleeding, so I was restrained. They then proceeded with a procedure that would relax me, but more so paralyze me. While in this state, I suffered a stroke and hemorrhaging on the brain. Upon those findings, they were unsure if I would ever be a fully functioning individual again. Once I was in full paralysis, the restraints were removed.

After delivering all of this information, they left the room. I felt so defeated. I could not believe all that my ears had just heard. I thought about me and only me, and my current state. My mom had quit working by this time, so she could be with me daily. As for me, I wanted God to just end it all right then. If I was going to lose all of my functions, and be unable to even hug my kid, I did not want this life at all. As much as I was loved, it still was not enough. Each day people came to visit me. Some people drove over an hour to come see me every day. The waiting room remained packed with friends, family, classmates, and neighbors. People could see me two at a time, between the hours of 8am-9pm. At this time, I had been hospitalized for over 30 days.

CHAPTER SIXTEEN

Pain and Suffering

Before people could come into the room to see me, my mom would prepare them. I looked nothing like me, and there were machines everywhere. My friend Crystal flew down to see me from Arizona. She determined in her mind that things were not that bad. When she walked in and saw the machines, she had to scoot around them just to see me. When she saw me, her knees buckled under her, and she almost fell. She was in complete shock and overwhelming emotions. She had no idea that my condition was that bad. Afterwards, more and more people were in shock. As they came to see me, emotions flooded the room, and they too passed out. Everyone was in shock. When I saw them though, I was so happy. I recognized their faces, and it felt so good to see them. I was literally smiling with my eyes.

I was well aware of where I was, and I missed my baby. I needed to see her. My mom kept me up to speed on her. She could look in my eyes and see that I needed to see her. She began to explain that my daughter could not come see me because we could not expose her to me just yet. She was afraid my baby would freak out. I understood her, but I was highly upset. I needed to see my child. Anytime she would mention my daughter's name I would begin to blink. She knew this was what I wanted but she did not think it was the best time. At this point, my daughter was my only reason for fighting. I was ready to talk, and I wanted to come off the trach that was in my throat. With the tracheostomy I was able to breathe through a tube. They began to take me off, but I had a panic attack and had to be placed back on it.

Crystal was flying in every two weeks and keeping me company. She was a skilled physical therapist, and she was very concerned about my paralysis. She began to talk to me about making small movements, and the idea of moving again remained dominant in my mind. Around this time, I hated when the hospital staff would come in to change me. It hurt so bad. The pain would be intense when they would turn me over. The worst part about this was, I could not express this at all. Once when they rolled me over, a tear began to fall from my eye. My aunt was in the room, and she witnessed it. My aunt then told my mom to not leave the room. When they turned me, I was crying and blinking. It was hurting so bad, and my mom saw me in pain. She asked them what was wrong with me, and they explained I had a "little sore." My mom got up to look for herself, and what she saw was horrific: my tailbone was showing.

They had been wiping me with baby wipes, and the slightest movement felt as if I had been shot. I was on a liquid diet; therefore, I was constantly urinating and defecating, and they were not coming to change me immediately. My butt burned intensely. My mom was panicking and very upset. She was told that I would have a certain type of bed that moved, so that we could avoid a bed sore altogether. I clearly did not have that. Crystal explained that they should have been moving me daily. I was in so much pain, and I just needed it to stop. Each night at 9pm my mom would leave, and as I watched her pack her things to go, I would begin to cry. I was aware of everything going on but could not communicate any of it. I was so lonely, and no one checked on me like they promised her they would. What my mom didn't know was that on the night shift, I was being mistreated.

CHAPTER SEVENTEEN

My Last Breath

After my mom would leave, I would remain awake all night. I watched the clock all night, waiting for 8am. The night shift nurses would leave me in urine and feces for hours at a time, with a stage four bedsore. There were possibly only two nurses who actually took care of me from the night shift. There were dozens assigned to me during my stay. There was one nice one that was so sweet during the day when my mom was there. One night she was working the night shift, so she came into my room. I was happy to see a familiar face that had been nice. By this time, I could move my lips, so I motioned the word, "Help." She looked at me and replied, "No." She then walked out of the room and closed the blinds. I did not get any assistance that night until 7am. All night I watched the clock as I burned in pain and cried. I felt so helpless. If there was a bottom beyond the earth, I felt that I was there. I had done nothing to anyone, but I felt hated, with no help.

Crystal had been coming every two weeks like clockwork. She began to work my fingers and legs. Each day she was there she would ask me to move something, and I would get excited thinking this was the day, but nothing would happen. She instructed my mom to begin working with me when she could not be there. She told her to move my arms and do what she could to make me move. Crystal would come into my room, shut the door and begin to work with me. I could not respond very much, but I had this little noise I would make to respond to people. One day she came, and I was able to wiggle my index finger. I was so proud. I am left-handed, but it was my right hand that began to move. After this they placed the remote in my hand so I could push it for help. At this time, I still could not push the button. I was able to move my head, so they placed a bell by my head to call for help. When I moved my head, the bell would ring. When it came to the night shift nurses, I was only able to use my bell once. A nurse came in and turned it off.

As more and more disrespectful occurrences happened, the deeper I sunk into depression and feeling useless. One day I happened to wake up and my mom was there. She said, "I have someone to see you!" My baby Rylee walked in. She came and laid on me, and she asked the nurse if she could touch me. She began to ask questions, asking what was wrong with me. The nurse took her time to explain things to Rylee. She also wanted to know if I was going to remain in this condition forever. The nurse told her that only God knew that. Rylee stayed and talked to me. She gave me updates on school, and how she was doing. The nurse began to prepare my medicine and Rylee asked if she could help. I did not realize that this medicine would make me so sleepy. As a result of taking it, I went out. When I woke up, I was so angry. Rylee was gone. I began to have a panic attack. I missed my baby so much. This was the first time I had been so upset, and the first time I experienced a panic attack. I could barely calm down. After that visit, and the incident, Rylee came to see me every other weekend.

As I continued to progress, I was able to spell out words on an alphabet board. My mom would drag my hand over the letter, and I would press on the one I needed. The first word I was able to spell out was "Help." My mom asked, "Do you need help?" I told her "No." I then spelled out the word "Night." She then realized I was trying to tell her I needed help on night shift, hence I was being mistreated on night shift. She made a report to someone in charge, and I was then assigned to a specific nurse to assist me at night. My bedsore continued to get worse. They had only placed bandages and ointment on it. I was getting to a point where the hospital felt they had done all they could do. I needed to be transferred to a rehabilitation center. In order to be transferred I would need chemotherapy at the location prior to my arrival. Chemo is used to treat lupus and slow down the progression. Unfortunately, the chemo infusion did not arrive on time, and therefore I lost my bed there.

As a result of me losing my bed, the hospital still felt I needed to move closer to home. I was then sent back to the original hospital that I visited multiple times and had also failed to treat or diagnose me. Once I arrived there, all of my records were transferred with me, but I did not trust that they would do what was best at all. It was my first night there, and my mom left at 3am, but I felt very uneasy about being alone, so the nurse called and asked her to come back. I felt better when I saw her, and this particular morning she left the room to get something to eat. Every day I would take my medicine at 9am, but for some reason at this hospital the nurse on duty was moving slowly with my medicine. When my mom came back, she noticed I still did not have it and began to ask them to bring it. She kept calling them and they kept saying they were coming. The nurse did not arrive in my room until after 11am. Once she did arrive in the room with the medicine, she stood there and took forever to scan it and follow her procedure. I began to suffer a panic attack. My mom was telling me to calm down, but I could not. By this time my mom and the nurse were scared. The nurse began to buzz for assistance to come in. They brought in a bag to pump air into me, and I remember thinking about how hot the bag was. It made it even harder for me to breathe. My breathing became slower and slower, and I could hear my mom standing near the door screaming and screaming. She was asking them what was happening to me. I exhaled, very deep and long, and took my last breath.

CHAPTER EIGHTEEN

Not Time Yet

As I take my last breath......

10...... My breathing is getting slower and slower......

9...... The doctors are yelling, "Grab the oxygen!"

8...... My mother is yelling, "What's happening to my child?"

7...... I am looking at the ceiling, my eyes are slowly closing (going in and out of consciousness) ...

6...... I am thinking of my childhood, teenage years, and adulthood....

5...... All the plans I have ever made and all of the people I have not said goodbye to...

4...... I am now breathing slower than ever, and the breathing is deep while the exhales are long.

3...... I see all of my loved ones who have crossed over.

2...... I am yelling my child's name, as my spirit is lifted out of my body, I see my lifeless body....

1...... Deep exhale and then...Beeeeeeeeep

I felt myself levitate above my body. I could see myself. I was screaming my daughter's name. I continued to scream until I began seeing crystals. They were so beautiful. Everything was beautiful and it now had my attention. I stopped yelling. I felt peace come over me. I was now in another world, better yet another galaxy, and I felt so good and happy. I saw these spirits moving around, but everything was peaceful. Everything was perfect. I kept climbing to the top, but all of a sudden, I felt something like a hand on me, pushing me back. In a flash I saw my grandmother. She was sitting down at her picnic table wearing a red shirt and blue overalls, and she looked at me and said, "It's not time yet!" Next thing I know, I sat straight up on the table before they could say "clear," while still paralyzed and all. I saw them preparing to resuscitate me. Just as fast as I sat up, I laid back down, and they put me to sleep. When I woke up, the trach was back in, and I had a bath.

That night I rested, but I couldn't help but think that I was back at square one. I was no longer responding well to the feeding tube in my nose, my feeding tube was then moved to my stomach. I could not engage with the physical therapist there at all. The physical therapist would come and sit me up in a chair, and the bedsore continued to get worse. Since I was in the intensive care unit though, I was assigned to a caseworker. One day I heard my caseworker in the hallway saying something was not right. He began working to get me into the specialty hospital where I had previously lost my bed. He advocated for me to get out of that place. I finally got the news: after two weeks I would be leaving. I was not progressing there at all. I was so grateful for him, and until this day I credit him for being a part of saving my life.

When I arrived at the specialty hospital, I felt an overwhelming sense of peace. The goal there was to get me off the ventilator and begin the process back to normalcy. I was scheduled to be there for 13 days, but later I would be granted an extension and remain there for a total of 21 days. The staff worked extremely hard with me, and my insurance. I had experienced so much trauma. At the last hospital they would turn down my vent without me even knowing. This was their way of seeing if I could breathe on my own, but me not knowing was so scary. At the specialty hospital, they explained every move they made with me. I loved it. The others would only tell me once they saw me struggling to breathe. These people treated me like a human being and gave me a reason again.

I knew I was starting to feel alive and comfortable again, when I began wanting food. My mom came into the room one day eating Doritos. I wanted some so bad. She asked me if I wanted any, and I nodded my head yes. She allowed me to lick one, and my eyes became huge. She told me I could not have any more, because she might get in trouble. I found that funny. Around this time, I was finally able to get my phone back, and the first thing I did was check my bank account. I was in shock at how many funds I had accumulated. I had a rather sizable nest egg. It is amazing how much we can save when we are stationary. At that moment, I felt like I could actually stand to chill a little bit longer.

I could go on for days about how nice the staff was. I could tell they were genuine. I was assigned to a room with a bed that moved, like I was always supposed to have. The first night there, I slept like a baby. My body was so relaxed, and I felt so good. I could tell that this is where I needed to be to become whole again. I was finally receiving the correct therapy. Before, my body knew I was not in a safe environment. My parents thought I had given up when I did not respond to the therapist at the previous hospitals, but they were just not what I needed. Within the first week at the specialty hospital, I was standing, the second week I was making steps, and I came off the ventilator and the trach plus started eating actual food. I could not believe I was walking and eating. Soon, I was able to speak. I felt so safe. It was like my body knew it was time to work based on the environment I was in. They brought in a wound doctor who viewed my bedsore. They informed me that it did not look good, and I would need to have a debridement. By now I could not even lay on my back. The debridement procedure would include them cutting out the dead skin cells from the wound.

CHAPTER NINETEEN

Progress, Finally

Everyone was extremely curious as to how my bills were being paid. Rylee was able to help with some of that because she could get in my phone. My aunt was at my home, and she knew my mortgage was being paid, but she did not know how. It turned out that everything was on autopay. I was still earning all of my income. My sister was so unsure about it all that she created a Go Fund Me account. She knew I would not want that, but she was just not sure how things were going to be paid. I did not like people in my business, but I understood her heart. I first had to come off the trach that was in my throat, and in that moment, I could actually speak, and the first thing I said was "I'm stank." I truly felt so dirty. I had not had a good bath in so long, with good soap. My cousin brought some Dove soap, and my friend began to bathe me.

As great as the bath felt they were giving me, I continued to feel violated. There was no privacy left for me. People had seen and continued to see every inch of me. I felt so helpless about it all, and even more so I felt like a burden. I dreamed and longed for the day I could be in the bathroom alone again. When it was time to eat, I was beyond excited. My first meal was breakfast: pancakes, eggs, and bacon. It tasted so good. Even Though it was hospital food, it was still good. At this point, I was able to brush my teeth on my own. I had braces, and the various people I relied on to brush my teeth had been through the struggle. I truly appreciated everyone though. It is also funny how when people don't know your business, they sure will make up something. I was told that the rumor was I had contracted something overseas, which caused my decline. Little did they know I had been sick months prior to going on vacation. People are hilarious.

Once I was off the ventilator, I remained in the specialty hospital for three days, and then I was transferred to rehab. When I arrived at rehab it was nighttime. I was met by a nurse that meant to encourage me, but she was truthful. She told me the first three days would be the hardest in my life. She explained that the respiratory issues will be the reason. They told me they would not babysit me; I was going to have to work and work hard. She told me she was committed to me, and within the next few days I would be moving on my own. I went to bed anticipating what the next morning would bring. When I awoke the next morning, I got my meds, ate, and got dressed. They then placed me in a wheelchair. We arrived at the gym to begin therapy. It was not long before I understood what she meant: just everyday movement was extensive for me.

As I continued to move, it felt like my chest was on fire. I could not breathe. They kept reassuring me that everything was fine. They kept telling me that all of the feelings were normal. I was now dealing with my chest, exhaustion, and the bedsore was still causing me pain. I cried every day for the first three days. They were pushing me so hard and telling me I had to learn to do it on my own. They did not help me much when it was time to use the restroom, but they did monitor me. When I struggled, they assured me that it was okay. It was all pure hell, but tough love. The therapy included a room set up like a home. I had to show them my independence before I could leave. Because there were 16 steps in my home, I would need to climb 16 stairs. There was also a washing machine, a bed to be made, and other chores. I had to show that I could do it all.

My physical therapists were the best and they were so patient. There were times I would fall, and they would help me, and not delay me due to it. They did not want my stay to last any longer, and that could have been the penalty for me falling. My deadline to climb those 16 steps was November 3rd, and I knew I told my mom I wanted to be home before Thanksgiving. I was on a mission to get up those steps, and the third of November was heavy on my mind.

CHAPTER TWENTY

Dealing with the Mental Health

During physical therapy I had not yet gotten back on social media. People were sending me well wishes, so I responded "Thank you" under a post. From there people began to blow up the post. They were so happy to hear from me. I felt their love. It was so overwhelming to me, but at the same time it was everything to me. People truly cared for me. Some were people I had never heard of, loving on me. People believed so much in me, and wanted me to make it, including everyone from my hometown of Springfield South Carolina, my classmates (2007), my closest friends, and many more. This was just the drive I needed as I prepared mentally for the test. The day of the test, things got so hard. Every step I made, after making the first six, I wanted to be the last. I wanted to give up and just go back to my wheelchair. I was crying so bad and huffing and puffing. Once I was done, I could not believe that I had done it. I sat in my wheelchair, and just cried. I was going home.

After being severely ill, coding, losing over 50 pounds, and a terrible bedsore, I was going home. There would be no more hospitals. It was over. My mom, my best friend, and my daughter Rylee picked me up. We went straight to my house. I had not been home since my birthday, over three months ago. Once we pulled on the street, I saw my yard was filled with people. My aunts, cousins, my sister, and my dad. I got out of the car on my walker. I left it and walked to the front of the house and just looked up. I needed to take it all in. I looked at my house, and I began to just cry. My sister walked up to me and began holding me. I was so grateful. God had truly smiled on me. I was back! I had left on my birthday on a stretcher, in the same spot I was standing in. The Lord saw fit to bring me back full circle so I could stand there. I needed to be right there. I was so happy.

My support system has always been top tier. My Aunt Trell had moved into my home and had been caring for Rylee. Once we got inside, Rylee told me she needed assistance with her homework. I sat down to begin helping her like we had always done, but I realized I could not do it. I could not keep up, and I could not think it through like I used to. It was taking a ton of effort to help her, and it was draining me mentally. I started to rub my head, and I was stuttering which was a side effect of the stroke. I was hurt, because I could not do it. I could not help Rylee. I became frustrated, and it soon turned to anger. I lashed out at everyone in the home, including my mom. I was on so many antidepressants at the time, my emotions were everywhere. I was so sorry that I did that, and I let everyone know I did not mean it.

My aunt decided she could stay with us until I got back on my feet. She was an amazing caregiver; she even took care of my wound. I was scheduled to visit a wound center, and a wound vac was placed on me. This insured the wound did not become infected. They told me it would take a year for my wound to fully close. It was so deep and wide. My aunt continued to be the support I needed. She drove us everywhere. I had no idea how long it would take for me to become fully on my feet, everything depended on how my body healed. Aside from my aunt helping, I had a nurse coming in three times a week, and a physical therapist coming once a week. I believed in progression, so to help everyone along, I would take my walker down the street and see how far I could go. I walked daily.

It was not long before my trainer found out I was home. He told me I needed to get in the gym and do a 30-minute session with him daily to start working on my strength. He was very clear that I was not going to do anything too strenuous, but I needed to be there three to four times a week to get things back in motion. We began working, and I was determined. I had the time to focus on myself and was not scheduled to go back to work any time soon. I would spend time in bed and get up at times just to move around a little. I was told I needed to move as much as possible to ensure the wound healed. I also had to take in a ton of protein to increase my healing time as well. I started tapering off antidepressants. I had been so quick to snap on people and be mean to people who supported me. I would even break down crying for no reason. I had been on 42 different pills in the hospital, and at home I was on 34. My goal was to continue to decrease that number. I was not sleeping at all, and all of the trauma I had been through kept me upset. I went to the VA and told them I needed help. That day, they connected me with a therapist.

CHAPTER TWENTY-ONE

On Our Own

For two months I consistently went to my therapist. There, I allowed myself to express my feelings, and it felt good, because it was a no-judgment zone. I had so much frustration built up, but I knew if I expressed it, people would think I was ungrateful. I was tired of being treated like a handicapped, charity case. That was not who I was, and I did not want that to be my identity. Although I needed them, I hated feeling this way. I never wanted to offend them. I was able to let all of this out in therapy. The truth of the matter was: I was angry with myself. When I struggled to get back to who I was, it angered me because I felt as if these were things I had always done, so why could I not perform them now, or at least learn them again in a timely manner? I was frustrated with this. I also knew I needed to be better at receiving help from those who loved me. It was not their fault how I felt at all. I tried to become better all the way around, and release some of my anger.

Aside from being angry I was barely sleeping. I was having recurring dreams about everything I had been through. I knew I needed to dig deep into my psyche to figure out what was truly wrong with me, and honestly until this day I still do. The therapy during this time became a bit redundant. I wanted to totally open up, but I did not know how. I began to feel like I was saying what I thought I needed to say. I soon had enough of therapy and was pretty much done with it. After therapy I started itching back into some of my old routines. Nothing was ever resolved mentally unfortunately. I was excited about doing some of the things I used to do such as driving. One day I asked my aunt to allow me to try and she backed the car out of the garage so I could start the drive to my appointment. I drove down the street and to the stop sign that first day, and I became too exhausted. Everything felt heavy and numb. I stopped, got out, and allowed her to finish the drive. Each day we went out, she allowed me to drive, and each day I made it a bit further. Eventually I was fully back on the road. I was not going long distances, but I could go to Rylee's school and stores in the area. I was excited about being able to take Rylee to school.

My aunt eventually told me that once my wound healed, she would be leaving me and Rylee to it. I appreciated her so much for moving in to help us. As she said it was nearing the time for her to leave, I felt fear creep upon me. Rylee and I would soon be alone. For a while I had not had to worry about being prepared for school physically or academically.

When my aunt made the statement, I jokingly let her know I would miss her. My pride would not allow me to burst into the tears I felt burning behind my eyes. As my bedsore continued to heal, I knew the day was coming. She would no longer need to be there to change it. Eventually the day came, and she left. I cried terribly. I was so scared and so unsure of everything. Rylee was there for me, and my baby was so supportive. She literally became my little caregiver. If she heard any strange noise, or any irregularity she came running to see if I was okay. I knew my baby was a bit paranoid and suffered from the trauma as well. I did my best to keep her heart at ease about the situation. She was so patient with me, and truly became my shero.

CHAPTER TWENTY-TWO

Getting Back to Me

It soon came time for me to return to work. This was so hard and stressful for me, because six months prior to leaving I had been promoted, but I had forgotten all of my new duties. It was so frustrating having to re-learn it all. I have the most amazing co-workers and manager. They made learning everything again as easy as possible. They were patient with me, and just glad to have me back. When I walked in on my first day back, my desk was decorated, and there were sweet gifts waiting for me. This truly eased my mind that had become so overwhelmed. After a while though I came into my routines. I came to terms with the fact that my breathing would never be the same due to the scarring on my lungs. When I take deep breaths, my lungs don't expand as much. When I exercise, I am pushing things to the limit. I have always been a fighter, so I push through it. My breathing is normally all over the place. I frequently do sprints and other exercises to ensure they become stronger. I never desire to become lazy and not push myself. My body means a lot to me, and although I know my limitations, I don't allow them to limit me. The body can do miraculous things if you challenge it.

After my aunt left, there were times when I felt alone. These feelings had nothing to do with my family's support system, because they were amazing. This was all me. I wanted my family to believe I was truly getting back to me, although I was a long way from it. Until this day, there are things that trigger me. I literally have PTSD from what I experienced. There are days I feel like I am here on borrowed time. It's like at any moment things can drastically change as they did before. The mental health aspect of what happened to me is just so heavy. Sometimes I look at my skin and how dark it is. I look at the scars on my body, and I wonder if someone could ever love me with these inequities. I feel like there is so much baggage that will come with me, but trust me when I say I love me, I mean all of me! It is very hard for me to go back to who I was after experiencing things so life altering. I know my friends miss the old me at times, but this new me feels more right.

I am so "no-nonsense" now. No one will ever get over on me. There are times when I am not as nurturing as I should be, and I don't "baby" Rylee. I have to remember that she needs some of that for her emotional needs. I know that she knows that I love her, but I need her to feel it too. My support system is still amazing in spite of how I am. In return I try to make it to everything for everybody and sometimes I stretch myself a little thin. People always look forward to me hanging out with them, but sometimes I admit it gets overwhelming. I have so many groups of friends and I try to make time for everyone. I know how short life can be, and I don't want to miss anything. I know I need alone time, and time to sit with myself, but I rarely get it. I appreciate all of the love, I really do, but I know I need to establish boundaries. I do have a choice in the matter, and I cannot allow obligation force me to show up everywhere.

I still have all my bills set up on autopay. I am also working on other establishments to ensure that things are solid for me and Rylee if anything happens. I am taking all precautions so that she has a very easy, stress-free life. I don't want her worried or wanting for anything. Today when people with scleroderma ask me how I am able to move so well without any limitations, I explain to them how much I move around. I move my body and I stretch regularly. I have a burning desire to stay fit and I know that I cannot leave my body sitting. If I do that my skin will become stiff. By sharing my story and what I do, I have inspired so many people to get in the gym, become consistent, and get moving.

After coming home November 2022, my first trip was scheduled for June 2023. I was heading to Arizona to visit my best friend Crystal who had been by my side in the hospital. The one who slowly helped me began using my limbs again. By December 2023 I was headed out of the country to Curacao. The trip was beautiful, and I enjoyed every moment. This was my normal, and I needed it so much. In the midst of all of my living, I was invited to speak and share my story. It was an entrepreneurial brunch, and they wanted me to talk about business ownership and listening to your body in the hustle and bustle. I have been invited to speak at a few other events as well. I am certainly open to it, and I know the time is coming soon. My biggest goal now is to be a help to people. I want to serve God, and I want people to know that change is possible within their lives, they just have to see it and go for it. I want to continue to be a great daughter, mother, and a great friend. I want to be a great person all around. This experience taught me to listen more than anything else. Before now I was so reactive. When people would be talking to me, I would cut them off and continue their sentences. Now, I take the time and hear what they have to say, and I listen to understand. I also want people to know that when they have loved ones in the hospital, check on them regularly. Let these facilities know you care about your people. I can't stress enough how you must keep your body moving. If you ever find that you are in need of recovery, forget what the doctor's say, push yourself. Your body can do unlimited things you have never imagined it could. When you think you have nothing else left in the tank, there is always something else there. I can distinctly remember laying in that hospital bed paralyzed completely, and all I could think was "Girl you are going to walk again." I meant that I was going to walk, and I was going to push, and push myself, until my last breath.

THE END

Acknowledgements

Aunt Trell (Godmommy)- Thank you! Thank you for loving on my child and I! You uprooted and moved in my home to ensure Rylee made it to and from school each day, and you made sure she was fed, clothed, and her homework was complete. You took care of my baby, and for that you are golden. Because of you, she remained on schedule and received the level of love and consistency that we always maintained. Thank you for taking care of me day in and day out, when I arrived home. You then kept me fed, and well-taken care of. You changed my wound and were patient in my pain. Thank you for crying with me, listening to me vent, and reassuring me that I would be fine in no time. I love you!

To my immediate family-Aunt Ken, Uncle Ray, Uncle Linzy, Aunt Ruthamae, Jaz, Kendreanna, Keisha and family, Pat, Kia, John, Abby, my grandfather Jo Lewis, and more, thank you all so much for being there for me. I love you all beyond words, and I can't thank you enough for your sacrifices.

My Cousin Dee-You were by my side through it all! You made sure I was bathed, and that my feet were always in great condition LOL! I love you for that!

My cousin Shidaa-Thank you for loving me unconditionally. You prayed over me and was ready to fight for me. I needed your fire in my life. Thank you.

Trinity-My big baby! I love and appreciate you! Thank you for being there for me! It means the world to me!

<u>My Friends</u>

Crystal-You are best friend, traveling physical therapist, and so much more in my life. You played a major role in helping my body move again. You came from Arizona every other weekend just to move my body. I am almost in tears thinking of your love and dedication to me. You will always be key in my life. I love you.

Noel- My brother from another mother, you were there from the jump and the moment the ambulance arrived. You stayed by my side the entire time, and even documented my journey. Your footage will live on and serve as a testament to so many others. You have blessed me and the world. I love you much!

Adriana- My bestie who remained by my side. You spent the night with me, eating your snacks in front of my face! LOL! I forgive you sis! Love ya girl!

Koko-My best friend, thank you for your unconditional love and support! It means the world to me.

Shanta- My best friend, thank you for being there and making sure Rylee was good to go when school started. I did not have to worry about her clothes or shoes. You made sure things were done. Thank you from the bottom of my heart.

Celeste, Talea, and Dawn-My college sisters! Thank you for making sure I was always okay. Your check-ins were needed and will forever be near and dear to my heart.

Step and Quanda-My sisters from another mother! You all continuously prayed over me. You made sure my mom was good, and that meant so much. You rubbed oil in my hair, and just loved on me. I will forever be grateful for your kindness and care.

Shanesse-My sister from another mother! You made sure all the technicalities were taken care of. You ensured that my job paperwork was complete, and everything was up to date. You traveled for me even during your pregnancy and loved on me. I appreciate you. You are one of a kind.

The Ross family- I love you guys to pieces! Thank you for all the love and support! Thank you for always showing up!

Renee, Pam, Cynt, Shirley, and Melissa-Thank you for your support and unconditional love. It is much appreciated.

Precious- You came to sit with me in the mornings, and you helped bathe me. Thank you so much for being there and being a help to me. I will always be grateful.

Sham and Kendrick-Thank you for your support and love. It will forever be appreciated.

Constance-You checked on me and stayed overnight with me at times. Thank you for loving me this way.

Allie and Brandon- Family, you came to see me and made sure I was always good. I love you for this.

Keke- Thank you for your love and support! It means so much.

Felicia- Thank you friend, for being there! It is so appreciated.

Carla- My friend and former teacher who I love dearly! Thank you for continuously checking on me.

My hairstylist, Adrian- You loved on me and even cut my hair off when I came home because it was damaged due to the chemo treatments! You even bought me a wig and installed it. Thank you for making sure I was fly! I love you for this.

Clarissa and Kamaria-My sister/friend, you were my support system, and you were great at it. I appreciate your baby girl as well. Thank you so much.

Gio-Thank you "brudda" for the support. I will never forget it. Love you!

Jas Tilley- Sis, thank you for looking out for my family.

B. Card- Thank you for checking in, and making sure I stayed motivated as you continue to do. Thank you for just showing love.

The Unrivaled Fitness Family- Thank you for coming to the hospital and being so patient with working my body back into shape! Major thank you to Josh and Kaleigh.

The Class of 2007- You all came to see me at every hospital or facility and loved on me. You made sure I laughed and felt loved, and I felt every ounce of it.

The town of Springfield South Carolina- Thank you for all of your support and all the love shown.

To everyone I know, and those that I didn't know, THANK YOU! Thank you for all the love, prayers, support, calls, messages, and more! You all are the reason I kept going.

Contact Jvonne

Email: jvonnebelle@gmail.com

Facebook: Jvonne Belle